GW01396002

DISNEY

BABY MINE DUMBO 4

THE BARE NECESSITIES THE JUNGLE BOOK 6

BEAUTY AND THE BEAST BEAUTY AND THE BEAST 3

BIBBIDI-BOBBIDI-BOO (THE MAGIC SONG) CINDERELLA 8

BREAKING FREE HIGH SCHOOL MUSICAL 10

CAN YOU FEEL THE LOVE TONIGHT THE LION KING 16

CANDLE ON THE WATER PETE'S DRAGON 18

CHIM CHIM CHER-EE MARY POPPINS 20

THE CLIMB HANNAH MONTANA: THE MOVIE 22

COLOURS OF THE WIND POCAHONTAS 24

HAPPY WORKING SONG ENCHANTED 26

IF I DIDN'T HAVE YOU MONSTERS, INC. 28

LITTLE APRIL SHOWER BAMBI 30

SOMEONE'S WAITING FOR YOU THE RESCUERS 32

UNDER THE SEA THE LITTLE MERMAID 13

WHEN SHE LOVED ME TOY STORY 2 34

WHEN YOU WISH UPON A STAR PINOCCHIO 36

WHISTLE WHILE YOU WORK SNOW WHITE AND THE SEVEN DWARFS 38

A WHOLE NEW WORLD ALADDIN 40

YOU'LL BE IN MY HEART TARZAN ™ 42

YOU'VE GOT A FRIEND IN ME TOY STORY 44

ZERO TO HERO HERCULES 46

ZIP-A-DEE-DOO-DAH SONG OF THE SOUTH 48

HLE

HAL LEONARD EUROPE

LM £10.95

PUBLISHED BY
WISE PUBLICATIONS
14-15 BERNERS STREET, LONDON, W1T 3LJ, UK.

ORDER NO. HLE90003870
ISBN 978-1-84938-177-2
THIS BOOK © COPYRIGHT 2009 BY WISE PUBLICATIONS,
A DIVISION OF MUSIC SALES LIMITED.

MUSIC ARRANGED BY ZOE BOLTON.
MUSIC PROCESSED BY PAUL EWERS MUSIC DESIGN.
EDITED BY FIONA BOLTON.
PRINTED IN THE EU.

YOUR GUARANTEE OF QUALITY
AS PUBLISHERS, WE STRIVE TO PRODUCE EVERY BOOK TO THE HIGHEST
COMMERCIAL STANDARDS. THE MUSIC HAS BEEN FRESHLY ENGRAVED AND
THE BOOK HAS BEEN CAREFULLY DESIGNED TO MINIMISE AWKWARD PAGE
TURNS AND TO MAKE PLAYING FROM IT A REAL PLEASURE.
PARTICULAR CARE HAS BEEN GIVEN TO SPECIFYING ACID-FREE, NEUTRAL-
SIZED PAPER MADE FROM PULPS WHICH HAVE NOT BEEN ELEMENTAL
CHLORINE BLEACHED. THIS PULP IS FROM FARMED SUSTAINABLE FORESTS
AND WAS PRODUCED WITH SPECIAL REGARD FOR THE ENVIRONMENT.
THROUGHOUT, THE PRINTING AND BINDING HAVE BEEN PLANNED TO
ENSURE A STURDY, ATTRACTIVE PUBLICATION WHICH SHOULD GIVE YEARS
OF ENJOYMENT. IF YOUR COPY FAILS TO MEET OUR HIGH STANDARDS,
PLEASE INFORM US AND WE WILL GLADLY REPLACE IT.

WWW.MUSICSALES.COM

Beauty And The Beast

Lyrics by Howard Ashman. Music by Alan Menken

Blending traditional animation with computer-generated imagery, this is the only full-length animated feature film ever nominated for an Academy Award for Best Picture and the first film to receive three Academy Award nominations for Best Song, from which this one, sung by Celine Dion and Peabo Bryson, became the Oscar winner.

Hints & Tips: Make sure the quavers (eighth notes) are rhythmical throughout. Think carefully about the note your right-hand thumb needs to be on—it's not the same all the way through.

Smoothly ♩ = 80

Tale as old as time, true as it can be.

Bare-ly e-ven friends, then some-bod-y bends un-ex-pec-ted-ly.

Just a lit-tle change. Small, to say the least. Both a lit-tle

scared, neith-er one pre-pared. Beau-ty and the Beast.

Baby Mine

Words by Ned Washington. Music by Frank Churchill

This film, based on a book by Helen Aberson, tells the story of Dumbo, an elephant with extraordinarily large ears. This song plays during Dumbo's visit to his mother's cell, Mrs. Jumbo having been locked up after losing her temper with a group of children who were ridiculing her son.

Hints & Tips: A triplet is a group of three notes, equal in length, which are to be fitted into the time that two notes of the same type would take. Thus the three triplet crotchets used in this piece should be played in the time of two crotchets (equal to one minim).

The Bare Necessities

Words & Music by Terry Gilkyson

The Sherman Brothers were enlisted to completely rewrite the music for this animated feature, based on the book of the same name by Rudyard Kipling. Composed by long-time Disney collaborator Terry Gilkyson and sung by characters Baloo and Mowgli, this song was the only track to survive from the earlier, rejected draft.

Hints & Tips: Follow the words of the song to help you with the tied rhythms. 2/2 means two beats in the bar, but it's best to count four, and play much slower, until you know the music.

Look for the bare ne - ces - si - ties, the sim - ple bare ne - ces - si - ties,_ for - get a - bout your wor - ries and your strife. I mean the bare ne - ces - si - ties_ or Moth - er Na - ture's re - cip - es_ that bring the bare ne -

Bibbidi-Bobbidi-Boo (The Magic Song)

Words by Jerry Livingston. Music by Mack David and Al Hoffman

Whilst in New York on business, Walt Disney kept hearing a novelty song, 'Chi-Baba Chi-Baba', played on the radio and hired its three composers to write for *Cinderella*. Little surprise then that this similar song appeared in the film and became a hit single, most notably for Perry Como & The Fontane Sisters.

Hints & Tips: Practise the right hand separately until you are comfortable with the intricate crossing over of fingers the part requires. Keep your fingers curved and close to the keys to help ensure a smooth melodic line.

B♭
Sa - la - ga - doo - la means
F
men - chic - ka boo - le - roo, but the
G
B♭m
G
thing - a - ma - bob that does the job is
C
Gm
C
bib - bi - di - bob - bi - di - boo.
F
Sa - la - ga - doo - la men - chic - ka boo la
bib - bi - di - bob - bi - di - boo.
C
Put 'em to-geth-er and what have you got?
Bib-bi-di-bob-bi-di, bib-bi-di-bob-bi-di,
F
bib-bi-di-bob-bi-di-boo.

Breaking Free

Words & Music by Jamie Houston

At the climax of what the author describes as a modern adaptation of *Romeo And Juliet*, the main characters, Troy and Gabriella, audition for the winter musical in front of the entire school. Gabriella freezes when she sees everyone staring at her, but encouraged by Troy, she finds the courage to sing this song.

Hints & Tips: The chorus (bars 21–36) should be played with more energy than the rest of the song. Keep the L.H. light and bouncy and make sure the tempo doesn't drag when you get to the tricky corners in the R.H. (bars 23–24 and 31–32).

12
E♭
B♭/D
Cm
F
- 'rent than who we are.
Cre - at - ing space be - tween us till
15
A♭
E♭
B♭/D
A♭
we're sep - 'rate hearts.
But your faith, it gives
18
F/A
A♭
E♭/A♭
me strength,
strength to be - lieve.
We're
21
Cm
F
A♭
soar - ing,
fly - ing.
There's not a star in heav-
24
E♭
B♭/D
Cm
F
- en that we can't reach
if we're try - ing,
yeah, we're break-

Under The Sea

Music by Alan Menken. Lyrics by Howard Ashman

After a string of critical and commercial failures dating back to the early 1980s, this 1989 film, based on the Hans Christian Andersen fairytale, is given credit for breathing life back into the animated feature film genre and marked the start of an era known as the Disney Renaissance, or the New Golden Age of Animation.

Hints & Tips: There is a lot of syncopation in this song, creating a calypso feel. Mark in the crotchet beats with a line above the stave if this helps you keep your bearings, particularly in bars 22–23 where the right and left hands should move together.

o - cean floor.
Such won - der - ful things sur - round you.
What more___ is you look - in' for?
Un - der the
sea,
un - der the sea.
Dar - lin', it's bet - ter down___ where it's wet - ter, take___ it from

me.

Up on the shore they work____ all day;

out in the sun they slave____ a - way.

While____ we de-

-vot - in' full - time to float - in' un - der the sea.

Can You Feel The Love Tonight

Music by Elton John. Lyrics by Tim Rice

Signed by Disney to write the lyrics for this 1994 animated film and invited to suggest anyone in the world to write the music, Tim Rice selected Elton John. Strongly influenced by Shakespeare's play *Hamlet* and set in the Pride Lands of the Serengeti, the movie tells the story of the relationship between a lion cub and his father.

Hints & Tips: Most of the rhythms and fingerings in this piece are straightforward so take the opportunity to be expressive in your performance—think about phrasing (where to 'breathe') and dynamics. Listen carefully to the right hand in the chorus to ensure the two notes are sounding at exactly the same time.

Lyrics:
It's e-nough for this wide eyed wan-der-er, that we got this far. And can you feel the love to-night? How it's laid to rest? It's e-nough to make kings and vag-a-bonds, be-lieve the ver-y best.

Candle On The Water

Words & Music by Al Kasha & Joel Hirschhorn

Mocked by her father for her belief that her lover will return after being lost at sea for more than a year, Nora, played by Helen Reddy, sings this ballad from the balcony of the lighthouse in which they live, assuring his spirit that, though he may never return, she will never stop loving him.

Hints & Tips: Listen carefully as the right hand moves in thirds in bars 9–16 to ensure the two notes sound at exactly the same time. Also practise the chromatic passage in the left hand at bar 24 slowly until you are comfortable with the compacted hand position this phrase demands.

13 Am D Gsus2 G F Em F G
I'll paint a ray of hope a - round you, cir-cling in the air, light-ed by a prayer.
17 C Dm F G C Am F B♭ G E/G♯
I'll be your can-dle on the wa - ter, this flame in-side of me will grow. Keep hold-ing
21 Am C/G F C/E F G
on, you'll make it. Here's my hand so take it. Look for me reach-ing out to
24 C F Fm C F G C G
show as sure as riv - ers flow, I'll nev - er let you go.
28 F G C G F G C
I'll nev - er let you go. I'll nev - er let you go.

Chim Chim Cher-ee

Words & Music by Richard M. Sherman & Robert B. Sherman

Based on a series of books by P. L. Travers and starring Julie Andrews and Dick Van Dyke, the 1964 musical film *Mary Poppins* is thought by many to be the pinnacle of the Sherman Brothers' decade-long association as staff songwriters at Disney and the crowning achievement in Walt Disney's long career in the film business.

Hints & Tips: Place an emphasis on the first beat in each bar, especially in the left hand, to create a strong waltz feel to this jolly song.

18 Dm A Dm G Gm
Chim chim - i - ney, chim chim - i - ney, chim chim che - ree. A sweep is as
23 Dm E A Dm
luck - y as luck - y can be. Chim chim - i - ney,
27 A Dm G Gm
chim chim - i - ney, chim chim che - roo. Good luck will rub
31 Dm A Dm Gm
off when he shakes hands with you. Or blow me a
35 Dm/A A Dm
kiss, and that's luck - y, too.

FROM 'HANNAH MONTANA: THE MOVIE'

The Climb

Words & Music by Jessica Alexander & Jon Mabe

This ballad, from the 2009 musical adaptation of the US teen sitcom, laments the struggles of the double-life led by Miley Stewart as Hannah Montana, her popstar alter-ego. Home in Tennessee, Miley, played by Miley Cyrus, reconnects with a childhood friend and soon realises that her family life has been neglected.

Hints & Tips: Avoid the left-hand chords sounding too heavy by placing a slight emphasis on the first beat of each bar and playing the remaining three crotchets more softly. Listen carefully to ensure the two notes are sounding at exactly the same time.

15 C

There's al-ways gon-na be an-oth-er moun-tain. I'm al-ways gon-na wan-na make it move.

17 F   Dm   G

Al-ways gon-na be an up-hill bat-tle. Some-times I'm gon-na have to lose.

19 C

Ain't a-bout how fast I get there. Ain't a-bout what's wait-ing on the oth-er

21 Am⁷   G   F   C

side.   It's the   climb.

23

Colours Of The Wind

Music by Alan Menken. Lyrics by Stephen Schwartz

This was the first Disney animated feature to be based on a real historical character, namely the Native American woman, Pocahontas. It portrays a fictionalized account of her encounter with English settlers to whom, in this song, she tries to explain the wonders of the earth and nature, including the spirit within all living things.

Hints & Tips: Rather than keeping strictly to the tempo as you play this piece, achieve a relaxed, wistful feel by employing 'rubato'. This means you 'give and take', making some notes slightly longer than they should be and others a little shorter.

12 Em Am Em F C/E
you, but if you walk the foot - steps of a strang - er, you'll learn
15 Dm G C Em/B Am
things you nev - er knew you nev - er knew. Have you ev - er heard the wolf cry to the
18 Em F Am Em
blue corn moon, or asked the grin - ning bob - cat why he grinned? Can you
21 F G/F Em Am F C/E
sing with all the voic - es of the moun - tain? Can you paint with all the col - ours of the
24 Am Dm F C
wind? Can you paint with all the col - ours of the wind?

Happy Working Song

Music by Alan Menken. Lyrics by Stephen Schwartz

In this 2007 homage to conventional Disney-animated features, Giselle, an archetypal Disney princess, is forced from her traditional, animated Kingdom of Andalasia into the live-action world of New York City where urban vermin such as pigeons, rats and cockroaches respond to her call for help with the cleaning.

Hints & Tips: This song is based almost entirely on the scale of C major. If you practise this scale, both hands separately and together, you will soon find the melodic movement required in this piece much easier, as well as the slower-moving accompanying line.

If I Didn't Have You

Music & Lyrics by Randy Newman

After 15 nominations without a win, Randy Newman finally landed his first Oscar when this song, from the computer-animated comedy about a city of paranoid monsters who generate power from the screams of children, won the 2001 Academy Award for Best Original Song.

Hints & Tips: Play this song with a swing feel by making the first quaver in each pair slightly longer than the second. Try to listen to the original recording if you are unsure how this will sound.

13
F D G C
I would - n't have noth - in' if I did - n't have
1.
15
F A♭ E♭ B♭
you. Would - n't have noth - in' if I did - n't have,
17
A♭ E♭ B♭
would - n't have noth - in' if I did - n't have,
2.
19
A♭ E♭ C F
Would-n't have noth - in'… you.

Little April Shower

Words by Larry Morey. Music by Frank Churchill

The main characters in this 1942 animated feature film, based on the book *Bambi, A Life in the Woods* by Austrian author Felix Salten, are Bambi, a white-tailed deer, his parents, his friends Thumper (a rabbit) and Flower (a skunk), and his future mate Faline.

Hints & Tips: Watch out for the key changes at bar 9 and bar 17 and the numerous sharps in the intervening passage. Also follow the fingering carefully throughout, keeping your fingers curved and the pads of your fingers close to the keys.

Drip, drip, drop, lit - tle A - pril show - er, beat - ing a tune as you fall all a - round.

Drip, drip, drop, lit - tle A - pril show - er, what can com - pare with your beau - ti - ful sound.

Drip, drop, drip, drop. I'll nev - er be a - fraid of a

good lit - tle gay lit - tle A - pril ser - e - nade.

Someone's Waiting For You

Words by Carol Connors & Ayn Robbins. Music by Sammy Fain

Based on children's novels by Margery Sharp, *The Rescuers* tells the story of an international mouse organization dedicated to helping victims of abduction around the world, which, like the United Nations, has headquarters in New York. This song plays whilst such a victim is comforted by a shining star.

Hints & Tips: Keep the left hand relatively quiet as it bubbles along beneath the melody in this arrangement. Keep your wrist loose and rock gently between the notes.

faith lit - tle one   till your hopes and your

wish - es come   true.   You must try to be

brave lit - tle one.   Some - one's wait - ing

to   love   you.

When She Loved Me

Music & Lyrics by Randy Newman

The 1999 sequel to *Toy Story* again featured the secret adventures of a group of toys. Performed by Sarah McLachlan, this song is used for a flashback montage in which Jessie, a yodelling cowgirl, experiences being loved, forgotten, and finally abandoned by her owner Emily.

Hints & Tips: Think about the story this song tells and try to convey this in your performance using dynamics and rubato (see page 24). Sing through the song and match the phrasing you employ to create a similarly emotive rendition on the piano.

Through the sum-mer and the fall, we had each oth-er, that was all. Just

she and I to-geth-er, like it was meant to be.

And when she was lone-ly, I was there to com-fort her, and I

knew____ that she loved me.

FROM WALT DISNEY'S 'PINOCCHIO'

When You Wish Upon A Star

Words by Ned Washington. Music by Leigh Harline

Sung by the character Jiminy Cricket, at No. 7, this is the highest-ranked Disney song in the American Film Institute's *100 Greatest Songs In Film History*. The first seven notes of the melody have become an icon of the Walt Disney Company, even being adopted as the horn signal of the ships of the Disney Cruise Line.

Hints & Tips: Practise this piece slowly at first, paying close attention to the prescribed fingering. This will help steer you through the numerous accidentals and the often unusual intervals between notes.

Fate is kind, she brings to those who love

the sweet ful - fill-ment of their se - cret long - - ing.

Like a bolt out of the blue, fate steps in and sees you through.

When you wish up - on a star your dream comes true.

Whistle While You Work

Words by Larry Morey. Music by Frank Churchill

Following on from the success of their *Silly Symphonies* cartoon series, in 1937 Walt Disney Studios made this, their first full-length animated feature, based on the fairytale of the same name by the Brothers Grimm, beginning what is now considered to be the Golden Age of Disney Animation which lasted until the early 1940s.

Hints & Tips: Give the phrases in this song shape by placing a slight emphasis on the first beat in each bar. Ensure you 'play' the rests in the left hand to create a light, bouncy feel throughout.

A Whole New World

Music by Alan Menken. Lyrics by Tim Rice

Tim Rice took over as lyricist for this movie, based on the Arabian folktale *Aladdin's Wonderful Lamp* from *One Thousand and One Nights*, when Disney regular Howard Ashman died in early 1991. In 1993 this became the first Disney song ever to reach No. 1 on the US *Billboard* Hot 100.

Hints & Tips: Don't forget that the key signature is F major, which means there are B♭s to remember. Also notice that the left hand has important material as well as the right hand and try to bring this out, e.g. bars 10 and 18.

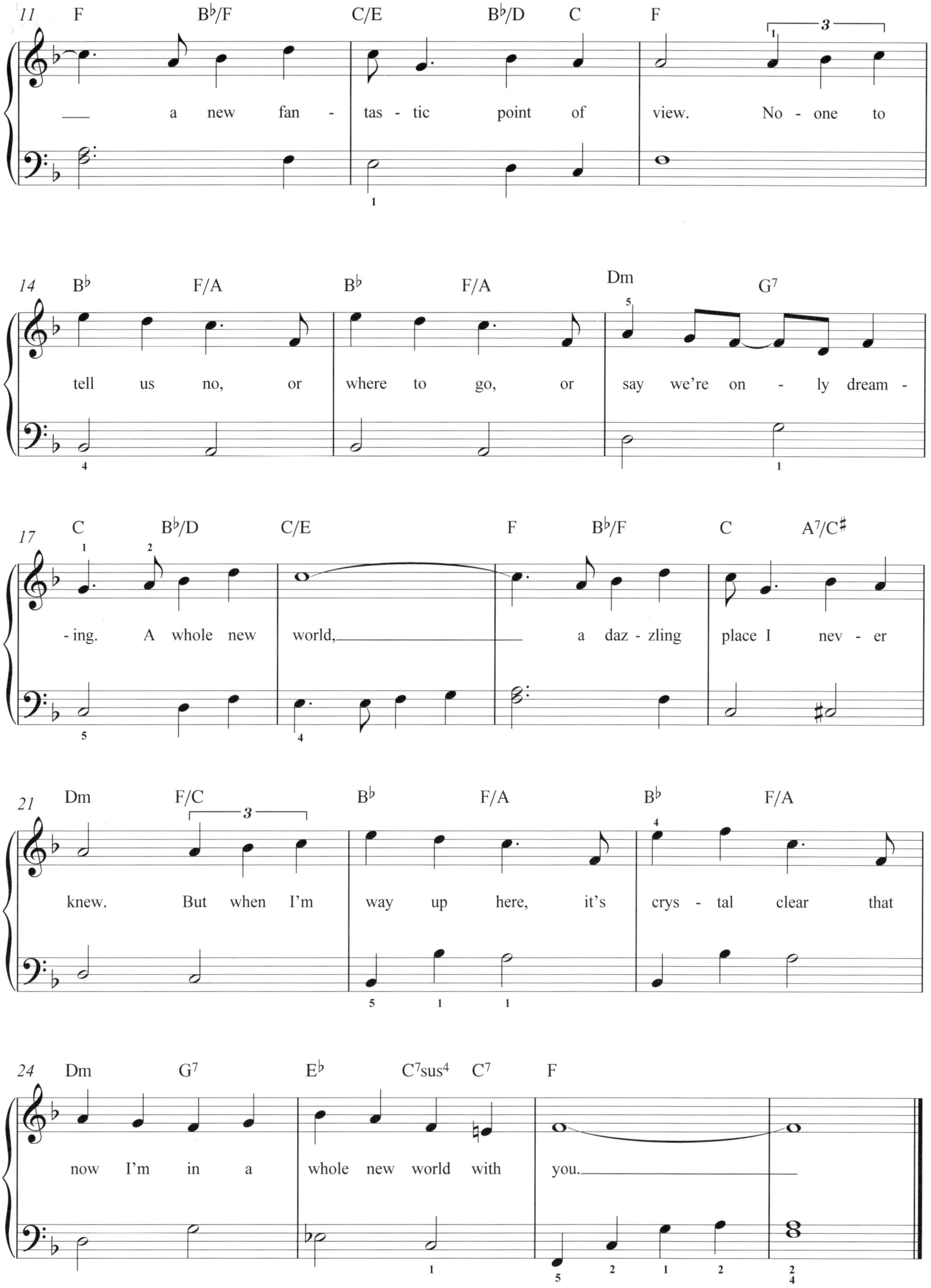

You'll Be In My Heart

Words & Music by Phil Collins

Based on Edgar Rice Burroughs' book, *Tarzan Of The Apes*, this 1999 animated feature is about a man raised by gorillas who has to decide where he truly belongs when he discovers he is a human. In this song the adoptive mother gorilla, Kala, sings that Tarzan should stop crying because she will keep him safe and warm.

Hints & Tips: Imagine the left-hand part is being played by an African drum, its steady rhythm underpinning the melody. Use a metronome to maintain a consistent tempo.

can't be bro - ken.   I will be here; don't you cry.   'Cause

you'll be   in my   heart.   Yes, you'll be   in my   heart.   From

this day   on,___   now and for - ev – er   more.

You'll be   in my   heart   no mat - ter what_ they   say.   You'll

be here   in my   heart   al - ways.

You've Got A Friend In Me

Music & Lyrics by Randy Newman

Composer Andy Newman established his trademark Pixar Animation Studios sound in this 1995 film about the secret life toys lead when people are not around, in particular that of cowboy Woody and Buzz Lightyear, a space ranger. It was the first full-length feature film to use only computer-generated imagery.

Hints & Tips: Play this piece with a gentle swing to capture the laid-back feel of the song, but don't become too relaxed—there are plenty of accidentals to keep an eye out for!

Some oth-er folk might be a lit-tle bit smart-er than I am, big-ger and strong-er too. May-be.

But none of them will ev - er love you the way I do,___ just me and you.

And as the years go by,___ our friend-ship will nev - er die.

You're gon-na see it's our des - ti - ny. You've got a friend in me.

You've got a friend in me.___ You've got a friend in me.___

Zero To Hero

Music by Alan Menken. Lyrics by David Zippel

Greek mythology became a new source of inspiration for Disney studios in this 1997 animated feature which tells the story of Hercules, son of Zeus, who is kidnapped by the evil Hades, Lord of the Underworld. Drained of all powers bar his strength, he becomes a hero by battling various monsters sent to destroy him.

Hints & Tips: This uptempo gospel number should have real pizzazz but try not to rush. Instead, listen carefully to ensure the left- and right-hand notes sound at exactly the same time, particularly where there is quaver movement in the left hand, e.g. bars 3, 7, 13, 15 and 17.

C E♭/F F E♭/F F C
He was a no - one, a ze - ro, ze - ro. Now he's a hon - cho,
E♭/F F E♭/F F C A Dm
he's a he - ro. Here was a kid with his act down pat. From
Gm F/A B♭ Bdim B♭/C F
ze - ro to he - ro in no time flat.
Gm F/A B♭ Bdim B♭/C F
Ze - ro to he - ro just like that.

Zip-A-Dee-Doo-Dah

Words by Ray Gilbert. Music by Allie Wrubel

This upbeat tune from the 1946 movie, based on the Uncle Remus stories about the adventures of Br'er Rabbit and his friends, was sung by James Baskett. He received an Honorary Academy Award for his performance 18 months after the film's release; the first man of African descent to win an Oscar.

Hints & Tips: Consider playing this short piece twice, employing a quieter dynamic (*piano*) the second time through and thus creating a contrast. Employ a crescendo in bars 9–12 leading into the jubilant ending.

456789
2/11 (177248)